HOW TO FIND ANYTHING ON THE INTERNET

A Kid's Guide to Safe Searching

by Ted Pedersen & Francis Moss

PRICE STERN SLOAN

To Michael Congdon,for his effort in making the *Internet for Kids* books happen, and, of course, to the kids (of all ages) for making them a success—T.P. & F.M.

Trademark Note: All terms mentioned in the book that are known to be registered trademarks, trademarks, or service marks have been appropriately capitalized. Price Stern Sloan cannot attest to the accuracy of this information. Use of a term in this book should not be regarded as affecting the validity of any trademark, registered trademark, or service mark.

ISBN 0-8431-7593-1 A B C D E F G H I J

Library of Congress Cataloging-in-Publication data available

CONTENTS

Preface: A Note to Parents

Since most Internet providers require that an adult sign up for the Internet service by pledging to pay monthly fees and other charges billed directly to a credit card, parents must be involved to a certain extent in their children's travels in cyberspace. And hooking up to the Internet involves using a modem, so unless you have a dedicated telephone line just for computer use, your phone line will be tied up whenever your kids are on the Internet. But parents have a lot bigger stake in their kids' involvement on the Internet than just money and telephone time. Like your cities and neighborhoods, the Internet is okay most of the time. But there are still a few hidden dangers to watch out for. Just as you teach your children to look both ways when crossing the street and not to accept rides from strangers, there are rules your children need to know and follow when they are navigating the Internet.

Think of the Internet as a giant shopping mall. There are places in the mall that are okay for your kids to go into and some places you've told them to stay away from. There are movies they can see, and movies they can't. As parents, you have set up rules, and you expect your kids to follow them. It's the same way on the Internet. And being online is a privilege that you've allowed your children.

If your kids' connection to the Internet is through a commercial service like CompuServe or America Online, you should know that the administrators of these services take reasonable precautions to keep truly objectionable or offensive messages off their systems. But once in cyberspace on the Internet, there are as yet no real barricades to keep children out of places they shouldn't be.

That's a bit frightening, and it's tempting to overreact—especially when you're facing a new technology that your children seem to understand better than you do. Perhaps the world has gotten more dangerous since you were a child, but that's no reason to stay indoors. What is needed on the street is street smarts. What you and your children need on the Internet is cybersmarts.

One risk you must consider: Your child may be exposed to inappropriate material of a sexual or violent nature, or receive harassing or demeaning e-mail messages.

A second risk is that your child might provide personal information while online that could risk his or her safety, or the safety of other family members.

To help restrict your child's access to areas on the Internet that contain inappropriate material, many of the commercial online services and some of the Internet gateway service providers have filter systems available to parents who wish to block out parts of the service they don't want their children to have access to. This is just like blocking out certain phone numbers or cable TV channels. If you are concerned, you should contact the Internet service provider you are using or thinking of using, by telephone or by e-mail, to find out how you can add these restrictions to any Internet accounts that your children use.

If either you or your child receives a message that is harassing, threatening, or sexually suggestive, forward a copy of the message to your Internet service provider and ask for their assistance.

Make it a firm rule that your children never, ever give out identifying information about themselves in a pubic online message such as a bulletin board posting or in a chat room. This includes their home address, last name, parents' names or workplaces, telephone number, and the name of their school. In fact, it is best that they never reveal this personal information online—even in e-mails to close friends—because there are some computer

hackers who can access even "private" communications between other users.

Ultimately, the best way to make sure that your children are having positive and safe experiences online is to stay in touch with what they are doing. Have them show you what they do, and ask them to teach you how to access the services they use. Keep in mind that while children need a certain amount of privacy, they also need parental involvement and supervision in their daily lives. Consider keeping the computer in a family room rather than your child's bedroom. That way you can all share the experience of going online. If you have cause for concern about your children's activities on the Internet, discuss it with them.

The bottom line is that it's up to you as a parent to set reasonable rules and guidelines for computer use by your children. On the following page, we've provided a contract for you and your children to sign. Copy it, fill it out, and put it somewhere near the computer so that your children will be reminded that they have promised to follow the house rules of surfing the Internet.

Make Internet use a family activity and you'll all enjoy it that much more.

Internet Contract

I, ______________, promise that I will surf the Internet for no more than ____ hours a day or a total of ____ hours per week.

I promise to keep my parents informed of all my activity on the Internet.

I promise to obey the following rules for surfing the Net:

Never give out personal information;

Avoid unpleasant situations;

Always be myself;

Always stick to my budget;

Always treat other online users with respect, as I would want to be treated;

Always use my common sense;

Be a responsible member of cyberspace.

I also agree to the following:

____

____

____

Signed: ____________________ Date: ______________

Signed: ____________________ Date: ______________

Signed: ____________________ Date: ______________

INTRODUCTION

The Internet and the World Wide Web are great places to hang out. You can browse exciting websites, chat online with friends, and play interactive games with someone who might be on the other side of the world.

In addition to being really cool and a lot of fun, the Internet is also an incredibly useful research tool. You can use it to find buried treasure! We don't mean chests of gold and jewels, but whatever in the world you're looking for. It might be the information you need to do a school report, or a clue to getting out of a softball hitting slump, or some tips on planning your family's summer trip to Yellowstone National Park.

Well, it really is out there on the Internet. Now, if only you can find it.

The good news is that the Internet is the largest library ever put together, and it's available to everyone who has a computer and a telephone. The bad news is that finding something on the Internet is like making a crash landing in the wilderness and trying to get home—without a map.

What's the difference between the Internet and World Wide Web? In the late 1960s, the Internet was created as a network of linked computers at various colleges and universities. Later, other computer networks all over the world linked into the system and it became the vast Internet that we know today. The *World Wide Web* (also known as the "Web") is just one part of the Internet, although it is rapidly becoming the most popular part. Today, the World Wide Web is made up of more than 250 million websites.

Imagine the Internet as a vast, unexplored jungle. Now imagine yourself about to enter that uncharted jungle in search of a lost treasure. The Internet today is a wonderful place that contains information on almost everything you ever wanted to know. But unfortunately, it is not very well organized.

If you were going to take a safari into the jungle, you'd hire a guide. (At least, that's what explorers always do in the jungle movies on TV!) So that's what we're going to do. In a way, this book will be your "guide to the guides"—an introduction to the most useful and fun search tools on the Internet, along with some tips on how to avoid getting lost or caught in quicksand.

CHAPTER 1

Navigating the World Wide Web

Let's meet two young cybernauts, Kate and Zach, who spend a lot of time on the Internet. Kate loves chatting with her friends and exploring the World Wide Web. Her younger brother, Zach, likes to play online games with fellow gamers all over the world.

Today we find Kate at her computer starting to do research for a school report about Ancient Egypt, and having trouble finding the information she needs on the World Wide Web.

"I don't want to know about Egyptian cotton," Kate complains to the computer screen. "I want to find out about Egyptian mummies!" She's been searching the Web for half an hour, using up most of her time allotment for the day. (Like many parents, Kate and Zach's mom and dad restrict the time they can spend online each day.) But she's having no luck even starting her search. "This box labeled *Search* on my ISP's home page is no help at all!" Kate complains.

ISP is shorthand for *Internet Service Provider*. Everyone needs an ISP to hook up their computer to the Internet.

Moments later, just as Kate is about to give up in frustration, a friendly figure pops up on her computer screen.

"CyberSarge!" Kate exclaims. "Where did you come from?"

CyberSarge salutes Kate sharply. "I told you I'd always be around when you needed me," he tells her. "And it looks like this is one of those times."

CyberSarge is an instructor at Cyberspace Academy, an online school where Kate and Zach learned about the Internet.

Now Kate notices that CyberSarge is wearing a pith helmet, khaki bush jacket, and shorts, like a safari guide. She says, "I like your new outfit."

CyberSarge nods thanks. "It really is a jungle out there on the Internet, so I'm dressing appropriately."

Kate nods in agreement. "It sure is. I thought I knew something about the Internet ... but I feel like a newbie all over again!"

Newbie **is just what it sounds like: someone who is new to the Internet.**

CyberSarge chuckles. "That happens to everybody," he explains. "The Internet is growing and changing so quickly that no one can keep track of it. And that makes finding things that much more complicated. Now let's see why you're having problems."

Kate points to the computer screen, where she's typed in the word *Egypt* in the search box on her ISP's home page.

Egypt | Search

"I'm looking for information on how mummies were preserved in Ancient Egypt, but I keep getting stuff I don't need," Kate explains to CyberSarge.

"Hmm ..." CyberSarge says, looking at the screen. "Well, part of your problem is you're using the wrong kind of *search engine*."

"Search engine?" Kate asks, puzzled. "What's that?"

"A search engine is a computer software program that collects and organizes websites so it can help you find specific information."

"It sounds complicated," Kate remarks, shaking her head.

"The best way to learn about search engines is to use them," CyberSarge answers. "So let's get started."

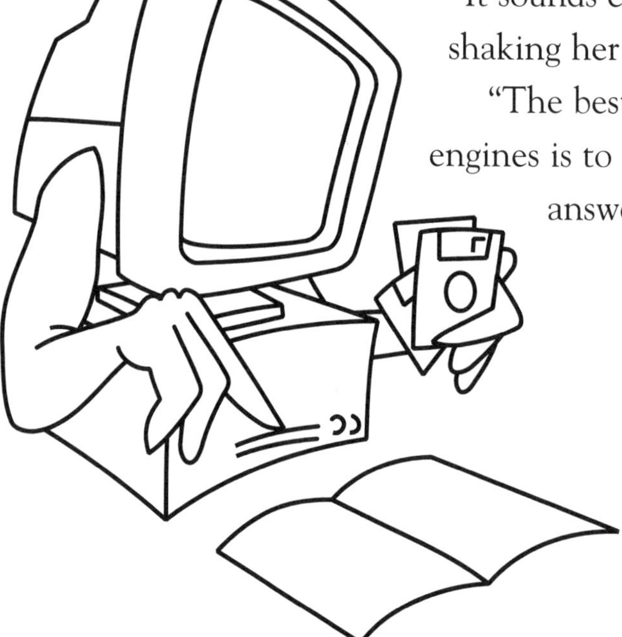

How Search Engines Work

If you've ever been on the Internet, you already know how fun it is to cyber-surf and explore new places. You can click on *hyperlinks* and jump from one web page to another.

> **A *hyperlink* (also called *link*) is the connection between one web page and another. When you click on a hyperlink (which is usually represented by underlined and/or colored text), you jump to a completely different web page.**

It's when you want to find something specific—like looking up information for that school report due Monday morning—that you realize how big the Internet is. And it just keeps growing! Millions of new web pages spring up every day, and even the most tireless web surfer couldn't possibly examine all of them.

Enter the search engine. It helps you sift through all those billions of words so you can find the specific information you need.

The search engine is your cyber–card catalog. When you go to your school library, you use the card catalog or computerized catalog to find the book you're looking for. The card points to a place on the shelf where the book is located.

The search engine, on the other hand, points you to the place (or places) in cyberspace where you might find the information you are looking for. And it also provides hyperlinks to those places so you can go and check them out.

Search engines are sophisticated software programs that catalog everything that's out there on the Internet in general, and the World Wide Web in particular. A little later in the book, we'll explain how they organize all this information. But for now, let's look at how these search engines collect their information.

The parts of a search engine that do the actual searching are called *spiders* or *software robots* (*bots* for short). These spiders or

Most search engine programmers name their bots. *Scooter* is the search bot used by AltaVista. HotBot's search bot is called *Slurp*.

bots are actually computer programs. Every minute of every day, thousands of these bots are cruising the Web, with no particular path in mind. They just browse around, following hyperlinks from web page to web page, all in order to check out what's new on the World Wide Web. The programmers who create these bots think of them as bloodhounds, sniffing out new web pages.

Bots perform thousands of hyper-jumps in a day. It's

tough work, but they are up to the challenge. Each time these bots find a new Web document, they make a copy of it and send the copy back to the main search engine. Then the bots continue to search for more new web pages. Meanwhile, back at the main search engine, the copy of the new web page is received, read, and filed away in the index or catalog, along with millions of other documents.

Every search engine has three major pieces:
1. The *spiders* or *bots* visit a web page, read it, and follow the links to other web pages.
2. The *index*, or *catalog*, is where the spiders deposit everything they find. Think of the index as a giant scrapbook in which the spiders paste copies of new web pages.
3. The *search engine program* is the software that sifts through the millions of cataloged web pages in its index to find matches to a search query.

So what does all this mean for you, the savvy web searcher? Well, here's where you come in. When you use one of these search engines to find information on the Internet, you type in *keywords* or a question. Then, when you hit *Search,* the search engine goes through its catalog, pulling out those documents that contain the same keywords. The closest matches are arranged into a list of *hits* which appears on your computer screen—a list of hyperlinks to those websites that (hopefully!) have some information you are looking for. So search engines not only give you a list of websites to try, but also provide you the cyber-paths to get there.

Keywords are those words you use to tell the search engine what kind of information you're looking for. If you're looking for a web page on baseball rules, then you might use keywords like "baseball," "scoring," and "rules."

A *hit* is the result of a search, when the search engine finds a web page containing the word or words you're looking for. Searching for the name of our president, William Jefferson Clinton, will generate tens of thousands of hits. Webmasters also use the term "hit" to count the number of visitors to their websites.

CHAPTER 3

All Search Engines Are Not Created Equal

Sitting at her computer, Kate nods as CyberSarge shows her the ins and outs of several search engines. "Some are better at your kind of search than others," CyberSarge tells her. "But we'll get into the particular ones later. First, let's define what your keywords will be."

"I know what keywords are," says a voice from behind Kate. She turns in her chair to see Zach, her freckle-faced younger brother, at the door to her room.

Zach's eyes widen as he sees their old friend CyberSarge on the computer screen. "CyberSarge!" Looking at his outfit, Zach asks, "Going on safari?"

CyberSarge salutes. "Afternoon, Zach. I guess you'd call this a cyber-safari. I dropped by to give your sister a hand. But it sounds like I won't be needed. Tell us what *keyword* means."

"A keyword is the word you type in the search box that tells a search engine what kind of information you're looking for," Zach explains.

"Can you show us?" CyberSarge inquires.

"Sure," Zach replies, squeezing into the seat next to his sister and reaching for the computer keyboard. "I need a new battery for my handheld game, so I type in the word *battery* and see what pops up."

CyberSarge nods. "That's a good start. But first, you need to know that all search engines aren't created equal."

"I always use the same search engine," says Zach. "What's the difference?"

"Let's take a look," answers CyberSarge.

Unfortunately, early spiders and bots weren't smart enough to figure out what was important in a web page, and what was not. So sometimes websites were indexed incorrectly, and searchers often failed to find exactly what they were looking for.

To make up for this, search site designers started using people instead of software robots to visit and categorize websites. Although much slower than computers, people were able to sort the sites they visited by categories and file them more accurately. These lists were all put together to make the second kind of search engine, called a searchable web directory, or just plain *web directory*. The most famous of these directory sites is Yahoo!

A web directory is like the index in the back of a book, which starts with the most general category, then moves to the more specific. For example, a main index category might be *Sports*. And under that main category there might be subcategories for baseball, basketball, football, and so on. Under these subcategories are sub-sub-categories, like the names of teams, or rules of play.

CyberSarge reaches down and clicks on the mouse. Soon a search engine home page pops up. "This is Yahoo! It's, one of the most popular web directories on the Internet," CyberSarge explains. "It gets millions of hits every day. People use it for everything from finding a new computer monitor to searching for the best deal on a new car."

Kate nods. "Mom and Dad used Yahoo! once to look for a Chinese restaurant when they went to San Francisco."

"Right," says CyberSarge. "Yahoo! has entire sections devoted to the largest cities in the United States. But it's better at finding the kind of information that Kate wants than the information that Zach wants." He motions to Zach. "Give it a try."

Zach scoots into the chair next to his sister and types in the phrase *rechargeable battery*. After a second, he gets two hits, but both are from the same site—a company in Hong Kong that manufactures lithium-ion batteries.

"That's no good," Zach says. "I don't want to read press releases. I want to buy a battery."

Kate takes over the keyboard. "Let me try

my search." She types in *Ancient Egypt* and is surprised by the number of hits she gets. "Wow! One category match, and one hundred and seventy-four site matches." She turns to CyberSarge. "What's the difference between a category match and a site match?"

CyberSarge points to the screen. "Like most web directory sites, Yahoo! is organized by categories, starting with the most general, and going to more and more specific subcategories. Look at how the category listing appears."

Kate and Zach look at the listing, which reads:

Yahoo! Category Matches (1-1 of 1)

Regional > Countries > Egypt > Arts and Humanities > Humanities > History > By Time Period

● **Ancient** History.

"This listing shows that Yahoo! has an entire category of websites that contain both your search words," CyberSarge says. "And see how the most general category, *Regional*, comes first, with the subcategories after it."

Zach points at the screen. "The search engine put your keywords *Ancient* and *Egypt* in boldface type," he says. "So that's a category match. But what's a site match?"

Kate already has that one figured out. "That just means that Yahoo! found websites listed under other categories with the words *Ancient Egypt* on them. Like this one," she says, pointing to the category:

Yahoo! Site Matches (1-19 of 189)

Health > Medicine > History.

...under which is a site listing:

- Medicine of **Ancient Egypt -** explores prescriptions, treatments, and cures.

Kate grins as she scrolls down the list of websites containing her keywords, *Ancient Egypt*. "I know I'll find what I'm looking for here!" she exclaims.

CyberSarge nods in agreement. "And don't forget, every one of those sites will have links to other sites—places that Yahoo! hasn't found yet—to help you in your search."

"But what about my batteries?" Zach complains.

"That's for our next trip through the wonderful world of searching," CyberSarge says.

CHAPTER 4

Two Types of Searches

The Web is potentially a terrific place to get information on almost any topic. Doing research without leaving your desk sounds like a great idea. But all too often, you end up wasting precious time chasing down useless *URLs*. Almost everyone agrees that there's got to be a better way! But for now, we can make the best use of the search tools that already exist on the Web if we know how they work.

URL (*Uniform Resource Locator*): Each document on the World Wide Web–each web page, each picture, etc.–has its own unique address in cyberspace. This address is known as a URL.

Keyword Searching

Keyword searching is the most common form of searching for text on the Internet. Most search engines do their text query and retrieval using keywords.

What are *meta tags?* A lot of web page formatting is invisible to the human eye, but not to the all-seeing bots that search engines send out. A meta tag is invisible to us, but it describes to the search engine what the site is about.

Sometimes the creators of a website specify the keywords for their site using *meta tags.* Otherwise it's up to the search engine to determine the appropriate keywords for that web page.

If keywords are not specified by the web page, the search engines pull out words that they believe to be the most important, and index the page accordingly. These are most often words that appear toward the top of a web page, or words that are repeated several times throughout the web page.

Search engines often have a hard time telling the difference between words that are spelled the same way, but mean something different—like a "hard" exam and the "hard"

drive on your computer. This can and does result in hits that are completely irrelevant to your query.

Some search engines also have trouble with so-called *stemming*. If you enter the word *bug*, should they return a hit on the word *bugged*? And what about singular and plural words? Or what about verb tenses that differ from the word you entered by having an "s" or "ed" on the end?

Most search engines also cannot return hits on keywords that mean the same thing, but are not actually entered in your query. For example, a query on *heart disease* would not return a document that used the word *cardiac* instead of *heart*.

Ranking the Results

When you run a search, you'll notice that the hits are often numbered in order, or (on some search engines) they have a

percentage assigned to them. What's the difference between those matches at the top of a search (or those with a percentage of 90 percent or so) and those which are not ranked so high? In general, these are the key factors that a search engine uses in ranking the results of a search:

- The number of search words matched; the more matches, the more relevant the results.
- Exact word matches, which are ranked higher than approximate word matches.
- Where the matches are located within the website. Closer to the top of the web page ranks higher than words found toward the bottom of the web page.

But searcher, beware! Because websites depend on search engines to guide you to them, website developers sometimes attempt to "trick" the search engine into giving them a higher ranking. Most search engines are influenced by the title of a web page. So webmasters may put keywords in the title of their website. Rather than calling her home page "Elena's Home Page," Elena names it "Elena's Dinosaurs and Baseball Page," which reflects her main interests. Or webmasters may "stuff" their pages with lots of different keywords. They can use meta tags to do this, or they can put the words on the web page as text that is the same color as the background color, say, blue on blue. You won't see the words on your web browser, but the search engine bot will! And as a result, the website may get indexed under several subjects it has nothing to do with!

As you can see, while keyword searching can be very helpful, it won't always result in the answers you seek. Later in the book, in the chapter called "Search Strategies and Tips," we'll show you how to prepare a keyword search so that you have the best chance of

Tip: Remember that the hits at the top of the list are picked by the search engine to be the closest to what you're looking for. But in case the search engine guesses wrong, it pays to check down the list to see if what you need is there.

finding what you're looking for. In the meantime, let's look at another kind of search that examines not just specific words, but what they mean.

Concept-based Searching

Unlike keyword search systems, concept-based search systems try to determine what you *mean*, and not just what you type. While a keyword search gives you exactly what you ask for, a concept-based search tries to figure out what you're really looking for.

Under the best of circumstances, a concept-based search returns hits on documents

that are about the subject you're exploring, even if the words in the document don't precisely match the words you enter into the search box.

Excite is perhaps the best-known general-purpose search engine on the Web that relies on concept-based searching. How does it work? Excite's software determines meaning by how often certain words appear on the web page, and where. When several words or phrases that are tagged to signal a particular concept appear close to each other in a text, the search engine concludes, by statistical analysis, that the piece is about a certain subject.

For example, the word "heart," when used in the medical/health context, would be likely to appear with such words as *coronary, artery, cholesterol, blood,* and so on. If the word *heart* appears in a document with other words such as *flowers, candy,* and *valentine,* a very different

context is established, and the search engine returns hits on the subject of love.

This often works better in theory than in practice. Concept-based indexing is a good idea, but it's far from perfect. The results are best when you enter a lot of words that relate to the concept you're seeking information about. For example, using the words *baseball, rules,* and *regulations* in a concept-based search is likely to turn up websites that explain how to play baseball.

CHAPTER 5

Search Strategies and Tips

Before you begin any search, it's important to give some thought to your search strategy. Do you just need general information on a fairly broad topic? For example, do you need to know the makeup of your state government, or how to play baseball? Or do you want more specific information, like finding out everything you possibly can about sprained ankles, or the e-mail address of a friend who's moved away to another city?

For the first kind of search, use a web directory. For the second, a search engine is probably a better choice.

Think of a web directory like the card catalog in the library. Not the computerized systems that most libraries are switching to, but the old-fashioned card files where you would find information by thumbing through the cards and searching for by the title, the author, or the subject. You would usually choose the subject option if you wanted to cover a broad range of information.

For example, suppose you want to create your own home page on the Web, but you don't know how to write HTML code, you've never created a graphics file, and you're not sure how to post a page on the Web after you write one. In short, you need a lot of information on a rather broad topic. Your best choice in this case is not to use a search engine, but a web directory. A directory probably won't give you anywhere near as many hits as a search engine will, but it's more likely to be on topic.

But what if you've tried looking through a web directory and that hasn't worked? What you're looking for is too specific, and it could take you hours—even days—to follow all the possible hyperlinks. In that case, you need the resources of a vast web index cataloged by spiders.

To find out about your favorite baseball team on Yahoo!, start by selecting the "Recreation & Sports" link, under which you'll find the subtopic "Sports." Click on that and you'll find another list of subtopics, including "Baseball." Click on that and select "Major League Baseball (MLB)", and then "Teams." From there, you can click on the team of your choice, like "Seattle Mariners," and get several websites to choose from—including the official site, player pages, and fan pages.

The next day, Zach is seated at the computer, still looking around in Yahoo!. But he's not having much luck. CyberSarge pops up on his monitor. "Getting frustrated?" he guesses.

Zach nods. "My friend Joey told me about an online store for rechargeable batteries, but he couldn't remember the URL."

"Remember, Zach, not all search engines are created equal," CyberSarge tells him. "In fact, your search is a bit more difficult than Kate's because there's so much more information available on Ancient Egypt than on rechargeable batteries."

CyberSarge clicks on the mouse, and a brand-new web page pops up: AltaVista. "This is one of the most popular search engines on the World Wide Web," CyberSarge explains. "That means that a lot of people use it to look for information on the Internet. So every website wants to be indexed here."

"Let's try it," Zach says, and types in the words *rechargable battery* in the search box. CyberSarge notices the misspelling of *rechargeable*, but he is too late to stop Zach before he clicks on the *Search* button.

But even with the misspelling, a page appears with the announcement: "AltaVista found 896 web pages."

CyberSarge laughs. "The people that develop these search engines are getting smarter. They know that the word 'rechargeable' is often

Some major search engines are also *portals*. A portal is your gateway onto the World Wide Web. Every major website, it seems, wants to be your personal portal. If you go onto the Web mostly to do searching, then having a search site as your online portal is not a bad idea. Tip: You can set your start page to be any web page you like. If your web browser is Microsoft Internet Explorer, for example, simply select "Tools, Internet Options." Then, under the "Home Page" section, type in the URL of the web page you want to appear every time you start up your browser. Click "OK" and you're done.

misspelled, and so they lead you to the right place even with the wrong spelling."

Zach notices that the page lists websites that seem to be what he's looking for, but he decides to start over. "I'll try it with the right spelling," he says, and types in *rechargeable battery*. This time, the results page reads: "AltaVista found 11,064 web pages."

"Think that's enough to get you started?" CyberSarge asks.

"I'll say!" Zach responds. "I could be searching forever!"

That's Kate's problem, too. Her search for *Ancient Egypt* on Yahoo! has turned up hundreds of sites, each with several links to dozens or hundreds of other sites.

But CyberSarge is there to help. "Having too many hits can be worse than not having enough," he agrees. "What you need to do is narrow your search."

"Let's do it," Kate says. "My report is due on Monday."

Narrowing Your Search

There are two different kinds of search: basic and advanced.

In a basic search, you just enter a keyword without choosing additional options.

An advanced search is most helpful when you are searching with several keywords. You can tell the search engine to pay more attention to one search term than to another, and to exclude words that might be likely to muddy the results. You might also search on proper names, on phrases, and on words that are found close to other search terms.

Some search engines also allow you to specify what form you'd like the results to take, and whether you wish to restrict your search to certain parts of the Internet—like the World Wide Web—or to specific parts of Web documents, like the title.

Tip: When you're looking for something in particular, try to make your keywords as specific as you can. If you're looking up "Michael Jordan," in addition to entering his name, include "basketball" and "Chicago Bulls." That way, you won't end up on the home page of Michael Jordan, the real estate agent in Miami.

Kate explains the topic of her school report. "It's about how the dead were buried in Ancient Egypt. I know they used a bunch of different chemicals and stuff to turn them into mummies, but that's about it."

CyberSarge nods as he looks at the computer screen. "Let's start by adding some more keywords to your basic search." He types in *Ancient Egypt burial mummies chemicals* and gets almost 62,000 hits! "That's still a lot," CyberSarge says, "but I think you'll find they're closer to your topic."

Sure enough, Kate finds an extensive University of Michigan site on Ancient Egypt, with an entire page devoted to burial practices. She reads: "They cut out the intestines, liver, stomach, and lungs and put them in jars. Yuck! Then they used this salt called natron to dry out the body."

CyberSarge makes a suggestion. "Let's narrow your search some more. Now that you have the name of a material used in mummification, try using the word *natron* in your search."

Using Quotation Marks

In the course of your exploration of the Internet jungle, quotation marks may just be the handiest search tool you have at your disposal. Let's see why.

Here's a phrase that most search engines hate: "Live long and prosper."

Most everybody knows that the phrase comes from *Star Trek*. So why do search engines choke on it? Because each of the words in the phrase is what is known as a *stop word*. Stop words will stop a search engine

***Stop words* are unimportant words too short or too common to be useful in a search.**

dead in its tracks and you will get meaningless results—like several million possible hits.

However, if you enclose a phrase in quotation marks, such as *"to be or not to be,"* it tells the search engine look for those words *only* when they appear together in exactly that order. Any search engine worth its salt will find a page that identifies the phrase as a famous line from *Hamlet*.

Here's another example. Suppose you're a science fiction fan and you want to search the Web for the home pages of all your favorite science fiction authors. If you simply enter the words *science fiction writer*, most search engines will return hyperlinks to all websites that contain the words *science, fiction*, or *writer*. This will probably include hundreds or even thousands of websites, most of which will have no relevance to your search. You will have to sift through all of those links looking for websites that contain all three words.

However, if you enter the words as a phrase enclosed by quotation marks (*"science fiction writer"*), you stand a good chance of getting some hits that deal with science fiction writing.

One piece of good news: Many search engines now automatically apply this use of quotation marks when searching on a multi-word query. But it's usually best to use them anyway, just in case your search engine doesn't have this feature.

Searching with Boolean Logic

"Some search engines employ a new technique, called *Boolean searches*, which we can learn about now," CyberSarge says.

"Sounds like *bowling*," Zach says.

"Boolean searches are named after George Boole, an English mathematician who in 1847, invented a system of logic that used *operators*," CyberSarge says.

"*Operators?*" Zach asks.

"These are connecting words you can use in a search to help make it more specific," CyberSarge explains. "The most common operators are AND, OR, and NOT."

Both Kate and Zach want to know how these operators are used, so CyberSarge suggests they do a search using them. "Try your *rechargeable battery* search using the search phrase 'rechargeable AND battery.'"

Tip: Some search engines recognize the symbols (+) and (-), which are similar to AND and NOT operators.

Zach does so—and is awestruck when the results page pops up: "AltaVista found 586,160 web pages." "Five hundred-eighty-six thousand!" Zach exclaims. "That's over fifty times as many as before!"

"Using the Boolean operator AND turns up sites where the word *rechargeable* and the word *battery* appear anywhere, not just together," CyberSarge informs Zach. "The operator OR would find sites where either the word *rechargeable* or the word *battery* appears. And searching with the phrase 'battery NOT rechargeable' would result in links to website about batteries, but not rechargeable ones. "

More Search Tips

Since the Web is vast and disorganized—and since search engines are still fairly new at cataloging all of this chaos—you need to take charge of your own searches. Here are some tips on how to make your searches most successful.

- **Try a specialized search engine.**

Besides the major web directories and search engines, there are lots of smaller sites that offer targeted searches in specific subject areas. For example, if you're looking for information about a specific movie star, the Internet Movie Database will get you the goods a lot more effectively than a general search engine like AltaVista will.

- **To cap or not to cap?** If you enter a keyword in lowercase, most search engines will find both upper- and lower-case matches. Use capital letters if you want an exact case match.

- **Choose your keywords carefully.** If you use a word that is very common, such as "baseball," chances are you will get an overwhelmingly long list of results. Try to pick less common words or use multiple keywords to narrow your search. Your best bet is to try three key-words per search.

- **Imagine the words on the page.** In picking keywords, imagine what words will be found on the pages you want.

Let's say you want to find out where the Super Bowl will be held in the year 2010. Instead of typing *Super Bowl locations,* you would be better off using *Super Bowl, 2010,* which would return web pages that have the words "Super Bowl" and the year in them.

- **Use wildcards.** Some search engines support the asterisk (*) symbol (known as the *wildcard*) to find variations on a word. For example, if you enter *cook**, you'll get pages about cooking, cooks, cookbooks—and probably cookies, too! Just be careful: While wildcards can be helpful, they can also return many more hits than you anticipated.

- **Read the help sections.** Most sites provide tips on using their particular service, although almost all of these primers could use a good editor and some more details. Still, it's worth reading these sections for sites you use often.

CHAPTER 6

Meet Some Popular Search Engines

Kate and Zach both end up getting the search results they were looking for. Kate gets enough information on mummification techniques in Ancient Egypt for her school report, along with her one-word summary: "Gross!" Zach finds a good source from which to order his rechargeable batteries and (with help from Mom and her credit card) is able to order them online.

But now both our friends are curious. How do they know what search engine to use for their next search? It's Saturday and Zach and Kate are at the computer when CyberSarge appears on their screen.

"Having trouble?" he asks.

"Not exactly," Kate replies. "We're just doing sample searches on different search engines, trying to figure out which ones are the best."

"But this could take forever!" Zach complains. "There are so many search engines out there, and running searches takes a ton of time."

CyberSarge agrees. "That's why I'm here," he tells the kids. "We'll take a closer look at the seven most popular search engines and learn how best to use each one."

Yahoo!

Location: http://www.yahoo.com

Yahoo! is an important Web resource. Technically, it's not a search engine, but a web directory that attempts to organize and catalog websites. Yahoo! also has search capabilities. Normally, when you search on Yahoo!, you are only searching through Yahoo!'s cataloged index of websites. If your search doesn't return any hits, Yahoo! offers you the option of using the AltaVista search engine to search the entire World Wide Web.

CyberSarge clicks on the mouse and a familiar red and white logo appears on the monitor. "Yahoo!" Zach exclaims.

"Yahoo! it is," CyberSarge says. "Do you know what kind of search engine it is?"

"Ummmm," Zach mutters, trying to remember.

Kate knows the answer. "Yahoo! is a web directory. It's like a catalog of sites on the World Wide Web."

"Right," says CyberSarge.

"I knew that," Zach says.

"What's Yahoo! best at?" Kate wants to know.

"Yahoo! covers lots of business sites, and has chat rooms. It even has regional versions, like Yahoo! Los Angeles and Yahoo! New York, which include restaurant and travel guides for those cities," CyberSarge replies. "But as with all directory sites, you have to remember, you're not actually searching the entire World Wide Web, but only the Yahoo! index."

"Just like a card catalog only lists the books in one library, not all the books in print," Kate offers.

"That's right," CyberSarge replies. "But unlike the library, Yahoo! will send you to other search engines if you can't find what you're looking for there. Let's go over Yahoo!'s main points as a search engine."

"It searches by keyword," Zach says, "and it organizes results from the general to the specific."

"Besides its own index, Yahoo! will look up e-mail addresses and search for newsgroups on the Usenet network," CyberSarge finishes.

"I like Yahoo! because it's easy to use," Kate says.

Usenet newsgroups are online bulletin boards, each devoted to a specific topic—from how to train your dog to the latest UFO rumors. There are over 40,000 different newsgroups on Usenet.

Yahoo!: Just the Facts

- *Types of search:* Keyword.
- *Search options:* Basic, Advanced.
- *Where it searches:* Yahoo!'s index, Usenet, e-mail addresses.
- *How it searches:* Boolean AND, NOT, and OR; or (+) or (-). Yahoo! is case insensitive.
- *Results:* Since Yahoo! returns relatively few hits (it will never return more than 100), it's not clear how results are ranked. Yahoo! tells you the category in which a hit is found, then gives you a two-line description of the site.
- *Help section:* Not very complete, but since there aren't a lot of search

options, detailed help files are not necessary.

- *What's good:* Easy-to-navigate subject catalog.
- *What's not so good*: Only a small portion of the Web has actually been catalogued by Yahoo!

AltaVista

Location: http://www.altavista.com

AltaVista was one of the first search engines on the Internet, and it remains one of the biggest and best. It's a fast, powerful search engine with enough special features to do an extremely complex search. But to use it to its full potential, you have to learn to use all its options. If you're serious about Web searching, mastering AltaVista is a good idea.

AltaVista not only lets you search the World Wide Web, but it also allows you to search for keywords in Usenet newsgroups.

To use AltaVista to search Usenet instead of the Web, select *Search Usenet* in the far right corner of the search box. By choosing Usenet, you will be searching through all of the messages posted on Usenet newsgroups in the past two weeks. The Usenet index is updated continuously, so articles are indexed within a few minutes after they are posted. If you want to find messages that were posted earlier than two weeks ago, you'll want to use the Deja News search, which we'll talk about later in the index of the book.

AltaVista's Usenet search has some special features that you might find helpful. You can find all the recent messages by a specific e-mail address by typing *from:username@address* in the search box. For example, *from:president@whitehouse.gov* would find all the messages posted by the President or his staff in the past two weeks.

You can search for all the messages containing a particular word or phrase by typing *subject: text* in the search box. For example, if you type *subject: "star wars"* you will find all the messages with the words "star wars" in the subject field.

You can find articles posted to a particular newsgroup by typing *newsgroups:groupname* in the subject field. You can use just part of the newsgroup name to match a range of newsgroups. For example, *newsgroups:la* will list all the newsgroups from Los Angeles.

What language is that? AltaVista has a special translation feature that lets you visit a foreign language website and have it translated into your own language. The translation is not totally perfect, but it works well most of the time. With so many websites available in foreign countries, this translation feature is a useful one.

"I liked the way AltaVista found all those rechargeable battery sites," Zach says.

"Especially once you figured out how to spell *rechargeable*," his sister teases.

"It was a typing error!" Zach protests.

CyberSarge laughs. "Correct spelling is definitely a requirement, even though a big search engine like AltaVista can sometimes make sense of common misspellings.

"AltaVista dates from the early days of the World Wide Web," CyberSarge continues. "It got started around 1995."

"That's probably why it turned up so many hits," Zach says. "It's been searching the Web for a long time."

AltaVista: Just the Facts

- *Types of searches:* Keyword, Questions.
- *Search options:* Basic, Advanced. Allows search refining, which means you can choose additional keywords and narrow your list of results even further.

- *Where it searches:* Web, Usenet newsgroups
- *How it searches:* Boolean AND, OR, and NOT, plus a new one, NEAR, which will find web pages in which the one keyword appears close to another keyword. Allows wildcards. You can decide how search terms should be weighted, and where in the document to look for them. Powerful search-refining tools, and the more refining you do, the better your results are.
- *Results:* Ranked according to how many of your search terms a page contains, where they appear in the document, and how close to one another the search terms are.
- *Help section:* Complete, but confusing. Too much thrown at you at once.
- *What's good:* Fast searches, capitalization and proper nouns recognized, large database, and a translation feature.
- *What's not so good:* Multiple pages from the same site show up too frequently.

Excite

Location: http://www.excite.com

Excite calls itself the "intelligent" search engine because of its concept-based indexing. While "intelligent" is an exaggeration, Excite is still one of our favorite search tools.

"I've used Excite before," Zach offers. "It's pretty good."

"For fun, let's try Kate's search again there," CyberSarge says, as the familiar Excite logo appears on the screen. Excite's search box is right at the top.

Kate starts to type in *Ancient Egypt*, but CyberSarge stops her. "One of Excite's main features is its advanced search page," he says. "Let's start there."

Clicking on *Advanced Search* brings them to a different page with three boxes in which to enter search terms.

"This is Excite's way of doing Boolean searches," CyberSarge says. "But they've already put in the operators, so you don't have to."

Kate reads: "'Include and/or exclude specific words or phrases in or from your search. Do NOT use quotation marks, modifiers like "+" and "-," or operators like AND.'"

"This is an example of concept-based searching," CyberSarge explains.

In the first box Kate selects "Results SHOULD contain the word(s) *Ancient*."

In the second box, Kate selects "Results MUST contain the word(s) *Egypt*."

In the third box, Kate selects "Results MUST contain the word(s) *mummy*."

Search

Results SHOULD contain | the word(s) | ancient | Search

Refine Search: Include and/or exclude specific words or phrases in or from your search.

Results MUST contain | the word(s) | egypt

Results MUST contain | the word(s) | mummy

Add more constraints

Do Not use quotation marks, modifiers like + and - or operators like AND .

"You can even add more of what Excite calls 'constraints' to narrow your search," CyberSarge points out. "But let's see how many hits you get with these."

The Excite search engine comes back with 4,080 hits. Kate reads: "'The total number of matches reflects the complete body of information that has been identified as relevant to your search from a pool of 50 million possible documents.' That's a lot of web pages!" Kate exclaims.

Zach points to the page. "And it says that the more words you add to your search, the more hits you might get." He turns to CyberSarge, puzzled. "I thought using an advanced search was supposed to turn up fewer results."

"Not necessarily," CyberSarge explains. "You might get more hits, but they're more likely to be *relevant* to your search, especially the hits at the top of the list."

Kate nods. "So refining my search might not get fewer hits, but the first ten or twenty will be closer to my topic."

"*If* you used the best search words," CyberSarge cautions. "It's a good idea to picture in your mind the kind of results you want. Let's use your search on Egyptian mummies as an example. Can you visualize the best page you could possibly find; one that has all the information you need?"

"I sure can!" Kate says excitedly. "It's got pictures of mummies, and burial instruments, and a step-by-step outline explaining how the Ancient Egyptians prepared the body for burial."

"Did you find that page?" Zach asks his sister.

"I got one almost exactly like that," Kate tells him.

Excite: Just the Facts

- *Types of searches:* Concept, Keyword.
- *Search options:* Basic, Advanced.
- *Where it searches:* Web, Usenet
- *How it searches:* Suggests you use more words, repeating key choices several times. Has recently added Boolean operators to aid in search refining: AND, OR, and NOT, and the symbols + and -.
- *Results:* Summarizes the most important sentences in the document.
- *Help section:* Very good. Includes a handbook that explains the Web, the software, the site, and how best to use it.
- *What's good:* Large index. Not quite as up-to-date as it could be. Excellent summaries.
- *What's not so good:* Does not specify

the format of the hits it returns, nor does it tell you upfront exactly how many hits there are.

HotBot

Location: http://www.hotbot.com

HotBot has become one of the most popular search engines. Its drop-down menus make it easy to select the kind of search you want, and it delivers very good results. HotBot is a good place to start with a general search inquiry.

It's Saturday. Zach is playing soccer and Kate, using her newfound searching skills, is helping her dad, Peter, in his office.

"What's the best search engine?" Peter asks Kate.

"It depends, Dad," Kate answers, feeling a little bit like CyberSarge as she answers questions that she was asking not too long ago. "What are you looking for?"

"I need some information on the latest in solar panel technology," Kate's father replies.

"HotBot is pretty good for technology

information," Kate tells him.

Kate loads the HotBot page and types in *solar panels*. She gets suggestions to look for books on solar panel technology at barnesandnoble.com, for jobs at CareerBuilder.com, or events at OnLive.com. In addition, HotBot has found eight sites, but none of them seem right.

Kate indicates a Lycos icon at the bottom of the page, next to HotBot's offer to get a "second opinion."

"Lycos is another search engine," Kate tells her dad. "It's pretty good with technology, too."

Kate clicks on the Lycos link, and the search is already completed by the time the Lycos page loads in the browser window. Peter notices a listing, "How Solar Panels Work."

"That sounds like what I'm looking for," he tells Kate. "Thanks."

HotBot: Just the Facts

- *Type of search:* Keyword.
- *Search options:* Basic, Modified, Advanced.
- *Where it searches:* Web, Usenet.
- *How it searches:* By phrase, by name,

and by Boolean-like operators in pull-down menus.

- *Results:* Pages with search terms in the title will be ranked higher than pages with search terms in the body text. Frequency also counts, and will result in higher rankings when search terms appear frequently in short documents than when they appear frequently in very long documents.
- *Help:* A FAQ (Frequently Asked Questions) section that answers users' questions, but not a lot of serious help files.
- *What's good:* HotBot claims to be fast.
- *What's not so good:* Some limitations on its Boolean-like operators, and the help files aren't very helpful.

The name Lycos comes from a Latin word meaning "wolf spider"—a creature known for seeking out its prey.

Lycos

Location: http://www.lycos.com

Lycos is one of the oldest search engines—up and running since 1994—and it continues to carry its weight. One of the nice things about Lycos is that it *reviews* popular websites as well as cataloging them. Lycos is also a good choice for finding images.

Lycos provides several web guides. These are similar to the directories in Yahoo!, but are not as extensive. However, these web guides can be helpful in that Lycos provides a minidirectory of the most popular websites. They also provide reviews of several of these websites, which can often direct you to a helpful website—or steer you away from one that doesn't fit your needs.

"So this is Lycos!" Zach exclaims as the Lycos logo appears at the top of the page. "It offers a lot of stuff!" He reads: "'Chat, Clubs, Email, Lycos Radio, Pictures, Build Home Pages. . . .'"

CyberSarge nods. "Like the other big search engines, Lycos would like to be your portal to the World Wide Web. They want you to set your web browser so that Lycos is the page that pops up when you turn it on. There's a lot of competition for your attention on the Web right now."

"That's a good thing, right?" Zach asks. "I mean, the more competition, the better each search engine has to be."

"That's the theory," CyberSarge replies. "But in practice, it can get confusing with all these sites clamoring for your attention. You have to work harder to keep from losing sight of your goal."

"So what does Lycos offer that the other sites don't?" Zach asks.

"Lycos is very good at finding images on the Web. It offers an image gallery of more than eighty thousand images—everything from glamour shots of Hollywood stars to artistic photos of old gasoline stations and cowboys. And then there's LycosZone, a kids' website with games, homework help, and a guide for parents and teachers," CyberSarge continues. "Lycos really tries to offer almost everything a web surfer might want."

Lycos: Just the Facts

- *Type of search:* Keyword, but Lycos is gradually becoming less of a search engine, it seems, and more of a Yahoo!-like subject index. Has recently had a cool graphical facelift. Proud of its ability to search on image and sound files.

- *Search options:* Basic, Advanced.
- *Where it searches:* Web, Usenet, News, Stocks, Weather, Multi-media.
- *How it works:* Lycos now has full Boolean capabilities (using choices on drop-down menus).
- *Results:* In a basic search, Lycos gives you the first 100 or so words on a web site. In an advanced search, you choose how you want the results to be listed—summary, full results, or short version.
- *Help:* Good, informative help screens are easy to understand.
- *What's good:* Large database. Comprehensive results given, including the date of the document, its size, and so on. Lycos lists the most popular web sites before the less popular ones.
- *What's not so good:* Doesn't rank results by relevancy and doesn't search Usenet newsgroups.

InfoSeek

Location: http://www.infoseek.com

InfoSeek is one of most popular search engines on the Web. In addition to its powerful search capabilities, InfoSeek has a very clean look and is easy to navigate.

"What's so great about InfoSeek?" Kate asks CyberSarge one afternoon as they search the World Wide Web.

CyberSarge points to the green logo at the top of the web page. "For one thing, it's part of Disney's go.com network, which provides InfoSeek with a lot of kid-friendly resources."

Kate clicks on the multi-colored *Kids* link with her mouse. A new page loads with more categories to choose from: *Stuff to Collect*, *Science & Animals*, *Search the Web*, *Play Games*, *Tons of Fun Activities*, and *Today's Surprise*.

"I see what you mean. InfoSeek has lots of stuff for kids," Kate says. "And a lot that's related to Disney movies and television shows."

"Kids who choose InfoSeek as their start page will have plenty to do," CyberSarge says. "In fact, there's so much, they might forget what they were searching for in the first place!"

InfoSeek: Just the Facts

- *Type of search:* Keyword.
- *Search options:* Basic, but powerful. The

site has an extensive catalog section for subject-oriented searching. You can also search for images.

- *Where it searches:* Web, Usenet, Usenet FAQs, Reviews, Topics.
- *How it searches:* Phrases, capitalization, no Boolean operators, but uses + and - instead (similar to AND and NOT).
- *Results:* Gives the first 30-100 words of the page, the URL, the size of the document and the relevancy score.
- *Help:* Good, useful.
- *What's good:* Fast, flexible, reliable searching. Allows capital letters and phrases.
- *What's not so good:* We're sure InfoSeek has some bad points, but we really can't think of any at the moment.

Ask Jeeves for Kids

Location: http://www.ajkids.com

Ask Jeeves for Kids is a search engine designed specifically for kids. It does not merely list the sites that may answer your question, but takes you right to the site, eliminating the frustrating search through countless sites which don't help you at all. In other words, you ask a question, and Ask Jeeves for Kids tries to answer it. In case Ask Jeeves for Kids can't answer your question, it also searches a number of other search engines.

CyberSarge has Zach's and Kate's full attention for their next lesson in searching.

"Ask Jeeves for Kids is one of the newer search engines and it uses something called 'natural language querying,' " CyberSarge explains. "That means you can type in a question at the search site using everyday language, just like you'd ask a question of a real person."

"You mean I can ask something like, 'Is Pluto the smallest planet?' and get an answer?" asks Zach, who's studying astronomy in school.

CyberSarge nods. "Right. You don't have to worry about things like keywords, Boolean operators, or whether or not to use quotation marks. The website's search engine takes care of that for you."

"How does it work?" Kate asks.

"The programming is pretty complicated, but basically it knows how most people ask questions, and looks for what it thinks are the important words in your question," CyberSarge explains. "But you'll understand it better if we go there and give it a try."

After a moment, a cartoon of a funny-looking man in an explorer's helmet pops up on the screen, along with a familiar search engine text entry box. "That funny-looking man in the helmet is Jeeves," says CyberSarge.

"Can we ask my question?" Zach requests.

"Sure. Type it in," CyberSarge replies.

Zach types in *Is Pluto the smallest planet?* and in a moment, another page pops up with a list of questions on it. Next to each question is a button to click on for more information.

- Is Pluto a true planet?
- What do the names of the planets and satellites mean?
- Where can I find an astronomy page about Pluto just for kids?
- Where can I find information for kids on the space topic Pluto?
- Where can I find general information on the celestial body Pluto?
- Where can I find a concise encyclopedia article on Pluto?

"Answering a question with more questions? That's not fair!" Zach objects.

"It's the way Ask Jeeves learns more about your question," CyberSarge explains. "Pick the question that's closest to what you want to know," he tells Zach. He clicks on the button next to the question about the astronomy page, and they jump to a page filled with useful information about stars, planets, and other astronomical things—including the answer to Zach's question: Pluto *is* the smallest planet in our solar system.

"Pretty cool!" Kate says. "Let me ask a question." She types: *Can a snake swallow a human being?* Soon, Ask Jeeves opens a page with several links about snakes—and a link to a page about swallows (the bird)! Kate, Zach, and CyberSarge have a laugh about that one.

"Natural language querying is still pretty new," CyberSarge tells the kids. "It's not hard to fool the program with words, like *swallow*, that have more than one meaning. But at least you get an idea of how it works."

CyberSarge continues: "Ask Jeeves has both its own data on questions that kids like to ask, and it also does a search on other websites, but it uses filters to screen out material that parents might not want their kids exposed to."

"Ask Jeeves is just about my favorite search site," Zach says. "I got an answer to my question right away."

Ask Jeeves for Kids: Just the Facts

- *Type of search:* Plain English questions.
- *Search options:* Basic, Advanced.
- *Where it searches:* Web.
- *How it works:* Ask Jeeves for Kids translates your question into a keyword search.
- *Results:* Will give you several possible search choices. You pick the one that best fits your needs.
- *Help:* Good, informative help screens are easy to understand.
- *What's good:* Very easy to use.
- *What's not so good:* Results can be somewhat limited.

CHAPTER 7

Megasearch and Metasearch Engines

A few days later, Kate and Zach are talking with CyberSarge at their computer. Kate is telling CyberSarge about how she helped her father do an Internet search for information on solar panels.

"HotBot didn't turn up the information that Dad was looking for," says Kate. "But then we tried Lycos, and he found the perfect website."

"Does that happen a lot?" Zach asks CyberSarge. "You start a search on one site but wind up going to another?"

"All the time," CyberSarge tells him. "With the hundreds of millions of web pages out there, no single search engine is going to

***Megasearch* vs. *metasearch*:** **These two words sound almost the same, but are really quite different. A metasearch lets you do a single search using several search engines—at the same time. A megasearch site is usually a website from which you can chose several different search engines—but in this case, you have to search each of them one at a time.**

find everything you look for. That's one reason the smart folks who think about the World Wide Web came up with *megasearch* and *metasearch* engines."

"*Meta* means 'above' in Greek," CyberSarge continues. "Think of a metasearch engine as one that stands above other search engines, examining the results of all their searches."

"How do they work?" Kate asks.

Clicking on the mouse, CyberSarge replies, "Let's find out."

After a brief wait, the first metasearch site appears: Dogpile.com. "Gee, look at all the other sites it searches!" Kate exclaims. On the screen, she reads: "'Dogpile searches LookSmart, GoTo.com, Thunderstone, Yahoo!, Dogpile Open Directory, About.com, InfoSeek, Direct Hit, Lycos, and AltaVista." She turns to CyberSarge. "I've never even heard of some of these search engines!"

"That's the Internet for you," he says. "There's something new every day."

Zach points to the rest of this list. "You can search newsgroups, check the weather, and even look up directions and phone numbers."

"And one funny thing," Kate notices. "The site is called Dogpile, so the button that is usually labeled *Search* says *Fetch*."

"What's the topic for our search?" Zach inquires, his fingers poised over the keyboard.

"I want to look up stuff on World Cup Soccer," Kate says. Zach types, and soon a long listing appears on the screen.

CyberSarge says: "You're bound to have thousands of hits with such a popular topic. But see how the results are organized."

"By search engine," Zach observes. "LookSmart found 76 documents, GoTo.com found ten, and Thunderstone found 2,732."

"And the button at the bottom of the page tells you that there are more search results from other search engines," CyberSarge points out.

"With so many, it's hard to know where to start," Kate says. "It's almost like eating too much dessert."

"Metasearch engines are probably more useful for topics about which you're having trouble finding information anywhere else," CyberSarge suggests.

Why use more than one search engine? The Web is growing so fast that even the best search engines can catalog only a small part of the information out there. AltaVista, for example, only catalogs about 18 percent of the Web. By using several of the top search engines, you can search about half of the Web. Different search engines also use different search methods, so the results from HotBot may be somewhat different from Excite's results.

Metasearch engines use their own spiders to search what other search engine bots have already collected. They query several search sites at once and then organize the results into a single list.

The good part about this is that you can get a lot of results in one place, but the bad part is that you will probably end up with duplicate links. Also, by doing a metasearch, you may not be using each individual search engine to its full potential. But, in spite of these limitations, metasearching can often be the quickest way to do a broad search.

Savvy Search (http://www.savvysearch.com) is another good metasearch engine. It allows you to enter your keywords or phrase and then proceeds to metasearch the indexes of the major search engines. Or you can link to one of the guides on the Savvy Search home page to narrow your search. For example, you can select to search only the Web or Usenet newsgroups, or you can pick specialty areas like *Health* or *Travel* or *Movies*.

But the best way to use the power of Savvy Search is to build your own customized metasearch engine. This is a simple three-step process:

- Select which of the 100 search engines to use.
- Give your personalized search engine a name.
- Finally, choose a start page category

that will automatically greet you the next time you return.

Although it's possible to turn on all 100 search engines, this is not a very good idea because you'll get a frightening number of hits. Review the list of possible choices and pick only those that seem most appropriate for your search. For example, if you're looking for historical information, then searching TV network databases of NBC and CBS probably won't be helpful.

Once you've made your list of search engines, you can then rank them.

- Rank a search engine **first** if the results from that search engine are very important to you. This instructs Savvy Search to give more weight to the results from that search engine.
- Rank a search engine **middle** if you don't want to designate the results of

this search engine as more or less important than the others.

- Rank a search engine **last** if you want to add this search engine but don't consider its results as important as the others you've selected.

CHAPTER 8

People Searches

In addition to the Web and Usenet, there are other parts of the Internet that you can search to find the information you're seeking.

For example, you might want to find out what your friend's e-mail address is, or reconnect with someone who's moved to another part of the country. The process of tracking this down is a little different from finding general information on the Web. Luckily, there are several special search engines that can help.

A few days later, Kate is on the Internet, reading her mail. She frowns as she reads a returned mail item in her Inbox. It's a message she sent to a friend, Annie, whom she'd met at summer camp. "I wonder why this didn't get delivered?"

CyberSarge pops up on the screen of Kate's computer to answer her. "It could be any number of reasons, Kate," he tells her. "Remember, cyberspace is still a pretty wild and woolly universe, and our e-mail messages are just bits and bytes of data, traveling in the electron stream. Lots of things can interrupt that flow."

CyberSarge peers at Kate's monitor. "Let's take a look at this e-mail to see if we can figure out what went wrong." He clicks the mouse and there, at the top of the returned message, is what looks like a secret code.

"What's that?" Kate wants to know.

"That's the *message header*," CyberSarge responds. "It contains information on what happened to this message on its travels. Most e-mail programs make it invisible by default, but there's usually a way to turn it on."

Here's what Kate's message header looked like:

Received: from localhost (localhost)
by avocet.prod.itd.myhost.com (8.9.3/8.9.3) with internal id SAC17676;
Sat, 19 Jun 2000 18:06:10 -0700 (PDT)
Date: Sat, 19 Jun 2000 18:06:10 -0700 (PDT)
From: Mail Delivery Subsystem <MAILER-DAEMON@myhost.com >
Message-Id: <199906200106.SAC17676@avocet.prod.itd. myhost.com>
To: <kate@myhost.com>
MIME-Version: 1.0
Content-Type: multipart/report; report-type=delivery-status;
boundary="SAC17676.929840770/avocet.prod.itd. myhost.com"
Subject: Returned mail: Cannot send message within 5 days
Reason: addressee unknown.
Auto-Submitted: auto-generated (failure)
X-UIDL: b0a548477858d080aee6e0e0d784c400

"There's my e-mail address," Kate says, pointing to the line that reads *To: <kate@myhost.com>*.

"Right. And there's the name of your Internet service provider's mail processing program, MAILER-DAEMON," CyberSarge says.

"What's all that other stuff? It looks like it's written in another languange," Kate says.

"Most of it is just identification and routing information for the message, so if anything goes wrong—"

"Which it did," Kate jumps in.

"—then you're able to find out, instead of never knowing if someone got your message or not," CyberSarge finishes. "And down here, you can see what went wrong. It says 'addressee unknown.' "

Kate is puzzled. "But I just e-mailed Annie a couple of months ago at this address. I know it's right."

CyberSarge rubs his hands. "What we have here are the makings of an Internet mystery: Where is Annie? And the first step is to double-check your typing of the e-mail address. Most undelivered mail is caused by typing in a '.com' when you mean '.net,' or spelling the e-mail address incorrectly. For instance, are you sure 'Annie' is spelled correctly?"

Kate nods, pointing to Annie's address in her address book. "The last e-mail I sent her went to annie_r@saturnnet.com."

CyberSarge nods. "But the mail came back marked 'addressee unknown.' Annie might have changed her Internet service provider. Or maybe her ISP was bought up by another provider. That happens all the time these days. So we need to take the next step."

"What is the next step?" asks Kate.

"Using a special World Wide Web search engine to find Annie," CyberSarge answers. He types in a new URL in the browser's address window;

Location: http://www.realwhitepages.com

http://www.realwhitepages.com, and a search site for BellSouth, a telephone company, pops up. "This is one of several *people searching* engines on the Web. Just type in your friend's name and see what turns up."

Kate types in Annie's name—and is surprised to see a whole list of names pop up. "There's more than one Annie, I guess."

"This often happens, especially with common names. Imagine what you get if you type in 'John Smith,' " CyberSarge says.

"The smart thing to do would be to check the snail-mail addresses of these Annies," Kate suggests.

"Good thinking!" CyberSarge congratulates her. "You're becoming a regular Internet detective." He clicks on the *Back* button on her browser. "But it's often faster to narrow your search here where you began, by typing in the city and state under Annie's name."

Kate does so, and is rewarded by a hit: annie_r@citysite.net. "There she is!" Kate exclaims. "She changed her service provider." Kate immediately starts to type Annie an e-mail message. "I'm going to get on her case for not sending me her new e-mail address." Then she turns to CyberSarge. "What if the BellSouth site hadn't turned up her address?"

"There are several other sites designed for people searching," CyberSarge tells Kate. "Bigfoot and Yahoo! People Search are two. There's another site, 555-1212.com, which offers a reverse directory. You just type in a telephone number and the name of the person appears. Click on the name and you can get their mailing address."

"Cool!" Kate says.

CHAPTER 9

Searching Newsgroups

Zach is browsing through a list of newsgroups, looking for one that deals with his favorite pastime: soccer. But there are so many newsgroups, some with odd names like *mpc.lists.freebsd.isp*, that his search is taking a long time.

CyberSarge pops up in his usual spot in one corner of the computer's screen. "Having some trouble, Zach?" he asks.

"I'll say!" Zach replies. "I'm looking for newsgroups about soccer, and even the ones with soccer in the name aren't covering the information I want."

CyberSarge clicks on the mouse. "What are you looking for?"

"I need new soccer cleats," Zach says. "The ones I have don't fit right, and I need to get another pair. I'd like some suggestions on which ones to buy."

"How are you searching?" CyberSarge asks.

"I just use my *newsreader* to sort out the titles of newsgroups with the word *soccer* in them," Zach explains. "I got about twenty." He starts to list them: "*alt.binaries.soccer, alt.games.soccer, alt.sports.soccer, rec.sports. soccer. ...*"

CyberSarge laughs and holds up his hand. "Stop! I get the idea." You're stuck in the Usenet swamp."

"Tell me about it!' Zach exclaims. "The newsgroups with *soccer* in their title are mostly about the Women's World Cup, or teams from England, or soccer movies. Everything but soccer cleats."

"Well, you need a better tool for the job," CyberSarge says, "and a website called Deja.com is a good place to start."

"What's Deja.com?"

"It used to be called DejaNews.com, and it was primarily a World Wide Web link to Usenet newsgroups. But now it's a whole lot more," CyberSarge explains as he clicks the mouse and the Deja.com website appears on the monitor. "Deja.com is a kind of home page

***Newsreaders* are programs similar to e-mail programs, except that they read messages that you select on newsgroups, then allow you to reply to those messages.**

for newsgroups, discussion groups, and chat about thousands of different topics."

"How does it work?" Zach asks.

CyberSarge points to the navigation bar. "Here are general topics, for searching. For more specific searches, type in the topic in the search text box."

"Just like in a regular search engine," Zach points out.

"Exactly," nods CyberSarge. "Except here you're not searching the Web, but newsgroups."

"So if I were trying to decide between a pair of Nikes or a pair of Adidas soccer cleats, I could check here to see what other people have to say about them," Zach says.

"Give it a try," CyberSarge suggests.

Zach types in the phrase *soccer shoes*, and it brings up several hits on various newsgroups. None is exactly what Zach is looking for, but one message mentions two brands of shoes Zach has never heard of before. CyberSarge points to a link at the bottom of the page, Track this thread for me. "What's a thread?" Zach asks.

"A thread is a group of related messages, or postings, on a particular topic," CyberSarge

Tip: You can use your web browser to read and respond to messages on Deja.com, which eliminates the need for using a separate newsreader program.

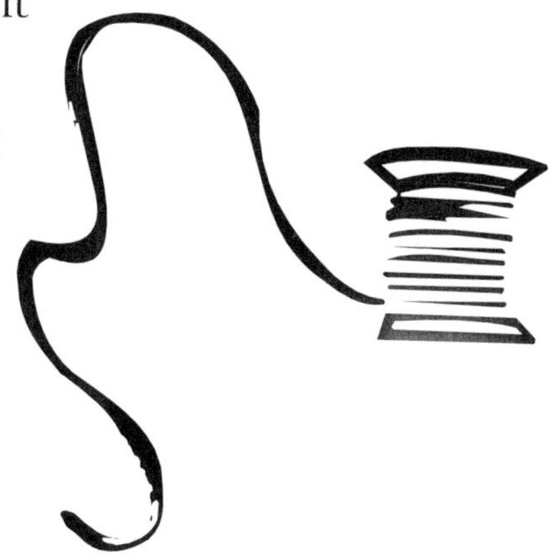

tells him. “If you click on this link, deja.com will keep track of this discussion for you and send you an e-mail when someone else posts a new message on this topic.”

Zach now has a new site to check back on, and some discussion groups that might be helpful in his search. “You really can find out just about anything on the Internet,” Zach says.

“You can if you know how to look,” CyberSarge adds.

INDEX

"Well, you've learned pretty much all I can show you about searching the Internet," CyberSarge tells his friends Kate and Zach. "You're on your own. But before I say good-bye, here is a handy reference list of all the search engines you might find useful." CyberSarge vanishes into the computer monitor, as Kate and Zach wave goodbye.

Major Search Engines

- **AltaVista** is at www.altavista.com. This is the granddaddy of all search engines and probably still has the largest catalog of websites.
- **Excite** is at www.excite.com. A smart search engine, and a good portal.
- **HotBot** is at www.hotbot.com. One of the best of the big search engines.
- **InfoSeek** is at www.infoseek.com. Now part of Disney's go.com network of Internet services.
- **Lycos** is at www.lycos.com. Another of

the big search engines.

- **Yahoo!** is at www.yahoo.com. Its easy-to-navigate catalog makes it one of the most popular online libraries.

Metasearch Engines

- **SavvySearch** is at www.savvysearch.com. You can customize this metasearch engine to fit your needs.
- **Mamma** is at www.mamma.com. Wants to be known as the "mother of all search engines."
- **Dogpile** is at www.dogpile.com. A very nice metasearch engine.
- **Metacrawler** is at www.metacrawler.com. It's customizable and has neat tools.

Megasearch Engine Websites

- **Internet for Kids** is at www.internet4kids.com. Click on the *Search Engine* icon to open our megasearch engine link page.

Special Search Engines

There are hundreds of specialized search engines that focus on particular subject areas. Here are just a few.

- **Amazon Books** is at www.amazon.com. While primarily an online bookseller, this is not a bad place to get information about books.

- **ABEBOOKS** is at www.abebooks.com. This is a database for over 4,000 independent bookstores, helpful in finding that out-of-print book.
- ***The New York Times*** is at www.nytimes.com. This is the home of *The New York Times* on the Web. In addition to current news, this site has a large archive of informational articles.
- **Deja** is at www.deja.com. This is where to go to search and subscribe to Usenet newsgroups.
- **Four11** is at www.four11.com. An online white pages directory.
- **Bigfoot** is at www.bigfoot.com. This is another website for conducting people searches. AT&T runs it and claims they have 90 million people in their database.
- **WhoWhere** is at www.whowhere.com. This is yet another popular people search engine.
- **Real White Pages** is at www.real whitepages.com. This is BellSouth's people finder website.
- **MapQuest** is at www.mapquest.com. Need directions or just a map of an area? Go here first.

- **Project Gutenberg** is at www.promo.net/pg. Here are some great works of literature, all of which are in the public domain.
- **Thomas Legislative Information** is at http://thomas.loc.gov. This is where you want to go to get information about Congress and the U. S. government.
- **Internet Movie Database** is at www.imdb.com. You'll find everything you ever wanted to know about virtually every movie ever made—right here.
- **Google** is at www.google.com. This search engine uses link popularity as a primary method of ranking websites. This feature can be helpful in finding those websites that have proven to be the most popular.
- **Northern Light** is at www.northernlight.com. This is a new and quickly growing website that is proving to be a favorite among researchers. Northern Light has a "special collection" of documents that are accessible to other search engines. Finding them is free, but there is a charge for viewing them.
- **Snap** is at www.snap.com. It has a human-compiled directory of websites in addition to a regular search engine.
- **About** is at www.about.com. About is a

web directory with a difference. There are guides maintained by real people in hundreds of subject areas.

Kids' Websites

- **Ask Jeeves for Kids** is at www.ajkids.com. A very smart search service, designed just for kids—but adults are welcome.
- **Yahooligans** is at www.yahooligans.com. This is the junior version of Yahoo!, and may be a better starting point for school-related searches than Yahoo!

These links will be updated, and new ones added, at our own website, www.internet4kids.com. You'll also find additional tips and tricks there for searching the Internet.

ABOUT THE AUTHORS

Ted Pedersen and Francis Moss are the authors of the internationally best-selling *Internet for Kids* books and *Make Your Own Web Page*.

Ted is the creator of the popular and award-winning *Cybersurfers* series, which has been translated into more than a dozen languages. He has authored fifteen kids' books, including *True Frights, Tale of the Virtual Nightmare*, and four *Star Trek: Deep Space Nine* young adult novels.

Francis is the author of *The Rosenberg Espionage Case*, a middle-grade book, and was a contributing author to *Using Windows 95*. He is webmaster of the popular Internet for Kids website at http://www.internet4kids.com.

In recent years, they have both been active as computer consultants and pioneers on the Internet, having developed several educational and commercial websites and interactive media projects.

More great PSS! titles for curious, young minds...

Internet for Kids

by Ted Pedersen and Francis Moss

ISBN 0-8431-7937-6

Look for a brand new edition

Summer 2001!

How to Make Your Own Web Page

by Ted Pedersen and Francis Moss

ISBN 0-8431-7459-5

Make your own place in cyberspace!

MY FAVORITE WEBSITES

Address	Notes